PROPERTY OF
THE PEOPLE WHO GET EDUCATION
DUVALL SCHOOL

PROPERTY OF
CHICAGO BOARD OF EDUCATION
DONALD L. MORRILL SCHOOL

THE CONSTITUTIONAL CONVENTION

PROPERTY OF
CHICAGO BOARD OF EDUCATION
DONALD L. MORRILL SCHOOL

Turning Points in American History

THE CONSTITUTIONAL CONVENTION

Martin McPhillips

Silver Burdett Company, Morristown, New Jersey

Cincinnati; Glenview, Ill.; San Carlos, Calif.;
Dallas; Atlanta; Agincourt, Ontario

Acknowledgements

We would like to thank the following people for reviewing the manuscript and for their guidance and helpful suggestions: David Williams, Professor of History, California State University; and Verna Mair, Library Consultant, Aldine Independent School District, Houston, Texas.

Cover: Painting of the Constitutional Convention courtesy of the U.S. Capitol Historical Society

Title page: Painting of the city of Philadelphia courtesy of the Historical Society of Pennsylvania

Contents page: Detail from John Dickinson's draft of the Articles of Confederation courtesy of the National Archives

Library of Congress Cataloging-in-Publication Data

McPhillips, Martin, 1950–
    The Constitutional Convention.

    (Turning points in American history)
    "Created by Media Projects, Inc." — T.p. verso.
    Bibliography: p.
    Includes index.
    Summary: Describes how delegates from the thirteen
original states came together in 1787 to create a
Constitution to preserve the newly born United States.
    1. United States. Constitutional Convention (1787) —
Juvenile literature. 2. United States — Constitutional
history — Juvenile literature. [1. United States.
Constitutional Convention (1787) 2. United States —
Constitutional history. 3. United States. Constitution]
I. Media Projects Incorporated. II. Title. III. Series.
KF4510.M35 1985   342.73'029   85-40169
ISBN 0-382-06827-0   347.30229

 Created by Media Projects Incorporated

Series design by Bruce Glassman
Ellen Coffey, Project Manager
Frank L. Kurtz, Project Editor
Jill Hellman, Photo Research Editor

Copyright © 1985 by Silver Burdett Company

All rights reserved. No part of this book may be reproduced or utilized in any form, or by any means, electronic or mechanical, including photocopying, recording, or by any information storage or retrieval system, without permission in writing from the Publisher. Inquiries should be addressed to Silver Burdett Company, 250 James Street, Morristown, N.J. 07960

Published simultaneously in Canada by GLC/Silver Burdett Publishers

Manufactured in the United States of America

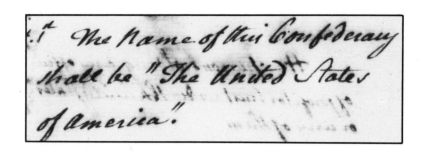

CONTENTS

INTRODUCTION

A TALE OF IDEAS

In 1787, when the Constitution of the United States was written, few political thinkers believed that the kind of government it created could survive. The republican form of government established by the Constitution was believed to be workable only in very small countries, if at all. How could it possibly hold together the thirteen original states with their great land mass and many different interests?

The men who framed the Constitution were aware of the belief that a democratic republic could not work. Rather than abandon the idea, however, they set out to create a system of government that would defy failure. In doing so, these men, the "Founding Fathers," asked themselves the most difficult questions about the nature of human life: Were people basically responsible, generous, and good, or greedy, selfish, and untrustworthy? Ultimately, they tried to build a system flexible enough for people to work and grow in but strong enough to control the ever-present human passion for power and domination over others.

This was no easy task. The men who gathered in Philadelphia in May 1787 were well educated in the law and in the history of government. They did not all share the same outlook. Some completely doubted the ability of people to govern themselves. Others believed the opposite—that the people, left to shape and decide their own laws, would act in a good and wise way.

Some of the most famous men in the history of the United States attended the convention in Philadelphia: George Washington, Alexander Hamilton, James Madison, and Benjamin Franklin among them. For three and a half months they wrestled with both the large structure and the small details of a constitution. They overcame

Thomas Hobbes (1588-1679), the English philosopher whose theory of government was based on his belief that humans exist in a "state of nature" and that government was needed to protect citizens from one another's greed and competitiveness

7

Historical Society of Pennsylvania

Pennsylvania State House (later renamed "Independence Hall"), site of the Constitutional Convention

many real political obstacles, solved many problems, and reached important compromises by which we are still governed today. In the end they had created a document that none of them loved without reservation but that most of them could support.

The test of a great historical effort is how well it stands up over time. The Constitution of the United States has endured a troubled infancy, a bloody Civil War, two great world wars, economic setbacks such as the Great Depression, the assassination or death in office of several presidents, and scandals and corruption at the highest levels of government. It is the oldest written constitution in the world, and the thoughts and decisions and events that shaped it make for one of the great stories of modern history.

UPI/Bettmann Archive

English philosopher John Locke (1632-1704). Unlike Hobbes, Locke believed that people were essentially good and well-meaning and that the happiness of individuals coincided with the interests of the community as a whole, or of the state. The writings of Locke, Hobbes, and other "Enlightenment" thinkers had been carefully studied by Thomas Jefferson, Alexander Hamilton, and other American Founding Fathers.

1

ORIGINS

The direct origins of the Constitution of the United States trace back to the year 1215. In that year, British lords and barons forced King John to agree to the Magna Charta, or Great Charter. This document guaranteed the British nobility that the king would not take their lands from them or collect taxes without their consent. It also guaranteed that trials would be decided by juries.

The Magna Charta was really a set of limitations on the sovereign power of the king. It said, in effect, that the king could rule England but that the nobles had certain rights that could not be violated. Over the centuries, this tradition grew in England so that these rights were gradually extended to common people as well.

The early British settlers in the New

A facsimile, or exact copy, of the original Magna Charta signed by King John in 1215. The document is in Latin and is bordered by the coats of arms of the English barons.

World brought with them the idea of the rights of Englishmen. In 1620, a group of religious outcasts—the Pilgrims—set sail from England for the New World. They landed at a place they called Plymouth Rock in an area that would eventually be named Massachusetts. Before they landed, they came to an agreement among themselves as to how they would enact laws that they would live by in their new settlement. This agreement took its name from the ship on which they were sailing, the *Mayflower*. Although the Mayflower Compact is not directly related—as a theory of government—to the Constitution, it did spark a tradition of self-government in the North American colonies of Great Britain.

The old tradition of the rights of Englishmen and the new tradition of colonial self-government, aided by the vast waters of the Atlantic Ocean, gave the American colonies unusual freedom from British control. It was these conditions in part that eventually stimulated the rebellion of the

UPI/Bettmann Archive

Library of Congress

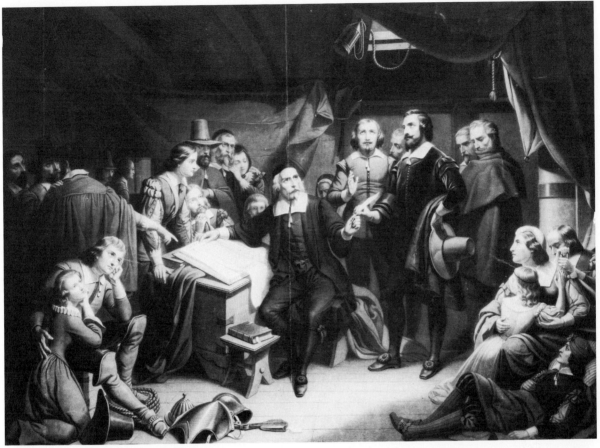

Signing of the Mayflower Compact, aboard ship, in 1620. The compact remained in force in Massachusetts for ten years and was the forerunner of other Colonial charters.

Colonies against Great Britain and allowed them to declare their independence from her.

During the Revolutionary War, both the Colonists and the British were motivated by a belief that their cause was just. The British held that the thirteen American colonies belonged to them, and that all

King John signing the Magna Charta at Runnymede, near London, as English nobles and churchmen look on

Colonists were subjects of the king. The king and the British Parliament constituted the supreme and legal government of the Colonies.

Before the Revolution, few if any Colonists questioned this authority. What caused the Americans to rebel was their feeling that their rights *as Englishmen* were being taken from them. The central issue was whether or not Parliament had the right to impose taxes on the Colonies without the Colonies' having the right to send representatives to Parliament. It was

13

By the King

A

Proclamation

for Suppressing REBELLION & SEDITION

George R

Whereas many of our Subjects in divers parts of our Colonies and Plantations in North America, misled by dangerous & ill designing Men, and forgetting the Allegiance which they owe to the Power that has protected & sustained them, after various disorderly Acts committed in Disturbance of the Publick Peace, to the Obstruction of lawfull Commerce and to the Oppression of our Loyal Subjects carrying on the same, have at length proceeded to an open & avowed Rebellion, by arraying themselves in hostile manner to withstand the Execution of the Law, and traiterously preparing, ordering and levying War against us. And Whereas there is reason to apprehend that such Rebellion hath been much promoted & encouraged by the traiterous Correspondence, Counsels & Comfort of divers wicked & desperate Persons within this Realm. To the end therefore, that none of our Subjects may neglect or violate their Duty thro' Ignorance thereof, or thro' any Doubt of the Protection which the Laws will afford to their Loyalty, We have thought fit, by & with the Advice of our Privy Council, to issue this our Royal Proclamation, hereby declaring, that not only all our Officers Civil & Military, are obliged to exert their utmost Endeavours to suppress such Rebellion & to bring the Traitors to Justice, but that all our Subjects of this Realm & the Dominions thereunto belonging, are bound by Law, to be aiding & assisting in the Suppression of such Rebellion, & to disclose & make known all treasonable Conspiracies & Attempts against us, our Crown & Dignity; & we do accordingly strictly charge & command all our Officers as well Civil as Military & all other our obedient & Loyal Subjects to use their utmost Endeavours to withstand & suppress such Rebellion & to disclose & make known all Treasons & traiterous Conspiracies, which they shall know to be against us, our Crown & Dignity; & for that purpose, that they transmit to one of our Principal Secretarys of State or other proper Officer, due & full Information of all Persons who shall be found carrying on Correspondence with, or in any Degree aiding this conflict that led to the famous speech by Patrick Henry, before the Virginia House of Burgesses, in which he declared there could be "no taxation without representation."

The Revolution was, therefore, not a war fought between two separate countries. At the outset everyone involved was an Englishman. The war started out as a conflict of ideas about what it meant to be an English citizen.

When the Revolution ended, in 1783, the Colonies became fully independent from Great Britain, and a new nation was already in the process of emerging. But by no means was it certain what kind of nation it would be. The thirteen colonies had each been separate political states that had joined together for the cause of independence. When the war was won, each former colony was essentially a sovereign state with its own government. The term "United States" referred merely to an association or confederation.

Under the Articles of Confederation, which had united the states during the Revolution, each state yielded certain powers to the "confederation," including the power to make treaties with other nations and to fight a war and to deal with the Indians on the western frontier. But no provision had been made to give the con-

King George III's proclamation "for suppression of rebellion and sedition" in the Colonies. The proclamation is dated August 23, 1775, four months after the first shots of the Revolutionary War were fired at Lexington, Massachusetts.

National Portrait Gallery

Patrick Henry

federation the power to use its authority. In other words, the Articles of Confederation granted to Congress certain powers but not the power of enforcement. It was as if a town had voted to buy its sheriff a gun but left out any provision for bullets. Each state was more or less free to do as it wished, restrained from doing so only by the good will that remained from the Revolutionary effort.

Each state had, in effect, more power over itself than the central government had by virtue of the Articles. This led to many problems, but these problems did not have an immediate impact on the states. The real concern of men like George Washington, Alexander Hamilton, and James Madison was that the future would bring much greater conflict. They feared that the states would drift apart—a process that was al-

Members of the committee who drafted the Declaration of Independence and presented it to the Continental Congress. Left to right are Thomas Jefferson, of Virginia, chairman of the committee and principal author of the Declaration; Roger Sherman, of Connecticut; Benjamin Franklin, of Pennsylvania; Robert Livingston, of New York; and John Adams, of Massachusetts.

ready under way—and that they would become rivals, if not outright enemies. In danger was the vision of one great nation working together to create wealth and preserve liberty.

Something had to be done. The great ideas of politics, from the Ancient Greeks on, needed to be considered and shaped into a framework of government that would last. Thirteen separate states must come together and create a power greater than themselves but a power that would not eliminate the states' own control over internal affairs.

16

When the Constitutional Convention (called the "Federal Convention" at the time) convened, in May 1787, what really began was a great adventure in ideas. How wise were the people? Did they possess a "natural" wisdom? Could they govern themselves under a democratic system? How could the many who were not wealthy and powerful be protected from the few who were? And how, in turn, were the interests of the wealthy to be protected from the envy and hostility of the less advantaged? Was a slave to be considered a person or property? Should a man have to own property in order to vote? Should there be a king, a hereditary monarch? If not, how powerful should a chief executive or president be? Should he be elected or appointed? Should he serve for a year or for a lifetime?

No one at the time was certain how any of these questions would be answered. The answers grew from debate about the nature of people and their governments. Were humans naturally good, or evil, or somewhere in between? Were people's rights natural—a gift from God or nature that no government could deny? Or were those rights strictly privileges granted by the ruling government?

The nation that was designed at the Constitutional Convention was far different from any that had come before. The ideas that shaped the Constitution of the United States of America are still a part of our everyday experience. They have helped define our way of life and have influenced the way in which we think about ourselves as individuals and as a people.

Pennsylvania Academy of the Fine Arts

2

A WEAK UNION

When the war between the new United States of America and Great Britain ended in 1783, the meaning of "united states" was not quite the same as it is today. The states were much more like independent countries than they were parts of a larger, unified nation. Each state was fortunate in having had experience in self-government. All thirteen had one form or another of a legislature that could make laws and raise taxes.

A number of factors held the states together, however, with at least the appearance of being a single nation. Together they had ultimately declared and fought for independence from Great Britain. Also, they had been regularly sending representatives to the Continental Congress in Philadelphia since 1774. And they had agreed to a pact of union—the Articles of Confederation.

On the surface, this all seemed a perfectly reasonable state of affairs. But below the surface all was not well. The states had been drawn together in a common cause against a common enemy. With the cause won, the states began to pursue their own interests with greater intensity. And just as each state's interests were different, so too were their ways of life. The most significant differences occurred between the northern and southern states—differences that eventually led to a bloody civil war.

One of the chief problems with the Articles of Confederation was that each of the states, large or small, had only one vote. For instance, Delaware, with a population in the year 1785 of about 60,000, had the same influence within the union as did Virginia, with a population of about 700,000. The people and their interests, therefore, were not represented equally. With the approval of nine states required to pass leg-

George Washington
(portrait by Charles Wilson Peale)

To all to whom

these Presents shall come, we the under signed Delegates of the States
affixed to our Names send greeting. Whereas the Delegates of the
United States of America in Congress assembled did on the fifteenth day
of November in the Year of our Lord One Thousand Seven hundred and
Seventy seven, and in the Second Year of the Independence of America
agree to certain articles of Confederation and perpetual Union between the
States of New hampshire, Massachusetts bay, Rhode Island and Providence
Plantations, Connecticut, New York, New Jersey, Pennsylvania, Delaware,
Maryland, Virginia, North Carolina, South Carolina and Georgia
in the Words following, viz. Articles of Confederation and perpetual
Union between the States of New hampshire, Massachusetts bay, Rhode Island
and Providence Plantations, Connecticut, New York, New Jersey, Pennsylvania, Delaware, Maryland, Virginia, North Carolina, South Carolina
and Georgia.

Article I. The Stile of this confederacy shall be "The
United States of America."

Article II. Each state retains its sovereignty, freedom and
independence, and every Power, Jurisdiction and right, which is not by
this confederation expressly delegated to the United States, in Congress
assembled.

Article III. The said states hereby severally enter into a firm
league of friendship with each other, for their common defence, the security
of their Liberties, and their mutual and general welfare, binding themselves to assist each other, against all force offered to, or attacks made upon
them, or any of them, on account of religion, sovereignty, trade, or any other
pretence whatever.

Article IV. The better to secure and perpetuate mutual friendship
and intercourse among the people of the different states in this union, the
free inhabitants of each of these states, paupers, vagabonds and fugitives
from Justice excepted, shall be entitled to all privileges and immunities of
free citizens in the several states, and the people of each state shall have
free ingress and regress to and from any other state, and shall enjoy therein
all the privileges of trade and commerce, subject to the same duties, impo-

islation, it was very difficult for Congress to get anything done. This was especially true because at different times individual states were absent from the Confederation Congress. So one or two states voting no could effectively veto a proposed action.

The Articles also had no provision for Congress to levy taxes, and so Congress could not pay even the debts that had been incurred during the Revolution. Nor could Congress borrow money. And those laws that Congress did pass it had no power to enforce. Enforcement was left to the states. There was also no method for settling disputes between the states. This resulted in the rise of trade barriers between individual states, and these barriers threatened the economic system of the new nation. In addition, the Confederation Congress was not able to conduct foreign affairs effectively.

Because of these difficulties, the time from the end of the Revolution in 1783 until the formation of a new government under the Constitution in 1789 is called the "Critical Period."

What is surprising about this time is that although there were signs of trouble, the states, on the whole, were not doing badly. Massachusetts and Connecticut were having a hard time economically, but most of the Mid-Atlantic and Southern states were fairly prosperous. Even more surprising, however, was that some of the

First page of the finished version of the Articles of Confederation, which went into effect in 1781

National Portrait Gallery

George Clinton, governor of New York and an early opponent of strengthening the central government

nation's most important leaders were not willing to leave well enough alone. They saw trouble on the horizon and were determined to do something about it.

The most important man in the United States at this time was George Washington. He was viewed with enormous affection by the people and was held in high esteem by leaders throughout the states. The argument for a more powerful central government was given strength by his support. Washington feared that under the weak central government of the Articles, the Confederation would lapse into a form of anarchy or tyranny, with states competing destructively in commerce and no provision for a unified defense against aggression from Europe—always a real possibility in those days.

Washington was, by any standard, an unusual man. He was not driven by ambition for power, as, for instance, Napoleon of France would be a few years later. Washington was a reluctant leader. He knew that one way or another he would be called on to lead the new nation, and he made it clear that he preferred to do so as the elected executive of a republic.

Washington was also acutely aware of how faulty and dangerous a weak union and an indecisive Congress could be. Dur-

Independence National Historical Park Collection

Thomas Jefferson, who was in Paris, as U.S. minister to France, at the time of the convention

ing the Revolution, he had had to lead a tattered, undersupplied army from battle to battle while constantly begging the Continental Congress for support. Rarely, in fact, did he get the support he needed. And rarely did his men and officers get paid. Near the end of the war he had used all of his influence to persuade his officers not to march on Congress to demand their back pay.

In spite of Washington's support, many leaders opposed a strong central government. This group, which included important and respected men such as Governor George Clinton, of New York, and Patrick Henry, of Virginia, believed that a strong national government would threaten the success of individual states. They feared that a national government would simply take up where Great Britain left off, imposing its will on states that were perfectly capable of governing themselves.

It was to the advantage of this antifederal group that there was no strong feeling of discontent in the country, no great outcry for central leadership. But men like Washington and Hamilton, who had been at the center of an arduous national effort—the Revolutionary War—feared the consequences of a weak central government. And they were joined by the likes of James Madison, a scholar of government and political philosophy, who understood that there had never been a revolution that did not lapse into tyranny (a formula that would presently be borne out in the French Revolution). There were good arguments for both national and state interests, and the compromise between these two points of view would become an essential ingredient in the new constitution.

It would be foolish not to recognize some of the positive accomplishments of the "Critical Period." Although the union was weak under the Articles of Confederation, it was far from crippled. The Congress was able to enact two major agreements establishing methods for dealing with frontier lands. The Land Ordinance of 1785 set guidelines for dividing and selling wilderness areas beyond the western boundaries of the states, and the Ordinance of 1787, also known as the "Northwest Ordinance," established standards for governing new territories. Specifically aimed at the territory northwest of the Ohio River, the ordinance provided for a governor and judges for each territory, and when the voting population of any territory reached 5,000, a legislature could be formed. The ordinance also outlawed slavery in those territories and encouraged the establishment of public education.

Important political accomplishments were made by some of the individual states. Virginia, for instance, passed a "Statute of Religious Liberty." This provided for freedom of religious expression and for separation of church and state. The author of the statute was Thomas Jefferson, author of the Declaration of Independence. The principles of the Virginia statute would later be incorporated in the Bill of Rights, which was added to the Constitution in 1791.

The Statute of Religious Liberty was important because during the Confederation there were still state-established churches. The guarantee of religious freedom in Virginia affirmed one of the founding principles of American independence—that people had the right to choose their own form of worship.

In the matter of slavery, a significant move forward was achieved in Massachusetts during the Confederation years. In 1783, the Massachusetts supreme court ruled that slavery had in effect been abolished by the state constitution of 1780. This was the first such action by a state that went against the widely accepted notion that human beings could be owned as property. It helped establish a standard that other Northern states would follow in the 1790s.

The weaknesses of the Articles of Confederation did not entirely prevent social and political progress. But by 1786, it was all too clear that the thirteen states were having problems conducting trade with one another. The year before, Maryland and Delaware could not agree on the rights of navigation on the Potomac River and Chesapeake Bay. The Virginia legislature decided that all of the states should meet to discuss problems related to trade. A convention was called for September 1786 in Annapolis, Maryland.

Only five states sent representatives to this convention, and no substantial work was accomplished. The one positive result was a call for another convention of all the states. The purpose of this convention would be to reexamine the Articles of Con-

New York Public Library

A dramatic—and imaginative—depiction of Shays's Rebellion, in western Massachusetts, January 1787

federation and recommend changes. The convention was called for the following year, 1787, in Philadelphia.

Again, at first, there was little enthusiasm for the idea throughout the states.

Then something happened that opened many eyes.

In the Massachusetts countryside, not far from where the Revolution began, unhappy farmers rose up in rebellion. The high taxes imposed on landowners to pay for the Revolutionary War effort had forced many farmers into bankruptcy and some into debtors' prison. Groups of farmers banded together and seized courthouses in parts of the state, to prevent the courts from confiscating their lands and also to protest the lack of paper currency with which to pay their debts. Then, in January 1787, some two thousand farmers tried to raid a government arsenal at Springfield, in western Massachusetts. They were led by Daniel Shays, who had been a captain in the Continental Army and had served at the battles of Fort Ticonderoga and Saratoga.

The rebellion sent a shiver of fear throughout the states. If such actions were to spread, how could they be put down?

Congress did not have the funds with which to raise a proper army. Was the chaos feared by Washington and others already rearing its head?

Shays's Rebellion turned out to be more symbolic of the potential for chaos than it was a real example of it. A volunteer army loyal to the government of Massachusetts quickly put down the rebellion. Still, Henry Knox, Washington's chief artillery commander during the Revolution and the first American Secretary of War, wrote a greatly exaggerated report of the uprising. He claimed that the rebels had massed a force of some fifteen thousand men. A sense of alarm spread up and down the confederation. Suddenly there was great enthusiasm for the convention of states that had been called for May 1787.

WE the People of the States of New-Hampshire, Maſſachuſetts, Rhode-Iſland and Providence Plantations, Connecticut, New-York, New-Jerſey, Pennſylvania, Delaware, Maryland, Virginia, North-Carolina, South-Carolina, and Georgia, do ordain, declare and eſtabliſh the following Conſtitution for the Government of Ourſelves and our Poſterity.

ARTICLE I.

The ſtile of this Government ſhall be, " The United States of America."

II.

The Government ſhall conſiſt of ſupreme legiſlative, executive and judicial powers.

III.

The legiſlative power ſhall be veſted in a Congreſs, to conſiſt of two ſeparate and diſtinct bodies of men, a Houſe of Repreſentatives, and a Senate; ~~each of which ſhall, in all caſes, have a negative on the other. The Legiſlature ſhall meet on the firſt Monday in December in every year.~~

*The legiſlature ſhall meet at leaſt once in every year, and that meeting ſhall be on the firſt Monday in December, unleſs a different day ſhall be appointed by law.

IV.

Sect. 1. The Members of the Houſe of Repreſentatives ſhall be choſen every ſecond year, by the people of the ſeveral States comprehended within this Union. The qualifications of the electors ſhall be the ſame, from time to time, as thoſe of the electors in the ſeveral States, of the moſt numerous branch of their own legiſlatures.

Sect. 2. Every Member of the Houſe of Repreſentatives ſhall be of the age of twenty-five years at leaſt, ſhall have been a citizen of the United States for at leaſt ſeven years before his election, and ſhall be, at the time of his election, an inhabitant of the State in which he ſhall be choſen.

Sect. 3. The Houſe of Repreſentatives ſhall, at its firſt formation, and until the number of citizens and inhabitants ſhall be taken in the manner herein after deſcribed, conſiſt of ſixty-five Members, of whom three ſhall be choſen in New-Hampſhire, eight in Maſſachuſetts, one in Rhode-Iſland and Providence Plantations, five in Connecticut, ſix in New-York, four in New-Jerſey, eight in Pennſylvania, one in Delaware, ſix in Maryland, ten in Virginia, five in North-Carolina, five in South-Carolina, and three in Georgia.

Sect. 4. As the proportions of numbers in the different States will alter from time to time; as ſome of the States may hereafter be divided; as others may be enlarged by addition of territory; as two or more States may be united; as new States will be erected within the limits of the United States, the Legiſlature ſhall, in each of theſe caſes, regulate the number of repreſentatives by the number of inhabitants, according to the ~~rate of one for every forty thouſand.~~ Provided that every State ſhall have at leaſt one repreſentative.

Sect. 5. ~~All bills for raiſing or appropriating money, and for fixing the ſalaries of the officers of government, ſhall originate in the Houſe of Repreſentatives, and ſhall not be altered or amended by the Senate. No money ſhall be~~ drawn from the public Treaſury, but in purſuance of appropriations that ſhall originate in the Houſe of Repreſentatives.

Sect. 6. The Houſe of Repreſentatives ſhall have the ſole power of impeachment. It ſhall chooſe its Speaker and other officers.

Sect. 7. Vacancies in the Houſe of Repreſentatives ſhall be ſupplied by writs of election from the executive authority of the State, in the repreſentation from which they ſhall happen.

V.

ſtruck out

3

THE FEDERAL CONVENTION

The delegates were scheduled to arrive in Philadelphia on May 14. In 1787, however, people did not have benefit of airlines, railroads, and automobiles. They traveled along terrible roads by horse-drawn coach or simply on horseback. So it wasn't until May 25 that enough delegates had arrived to begin the meeting. Even then, only nine states were represented, by a total of twenty-nine delegates.

The first day of the convention was marked by the election of George Washington to serve as the presiding officer. This laid a foundation of respectability for the work to be done. With Washington overseeing the debates, it was certain that they would be taken seriously by the delegates and that the results, whatever they might be, would be taken seriously by the people.

George Washington's working draft of the proposed constitution. Note that in this early form, the preamble lists the states individually.

Three days later the convention adopted rules. These were formal and business-like, with procedures adopted from the traditions of the British Parliament. For example:

"Every member rising to speak shall address the president, and whilst he shall be speaking, none shall pass between them, or hold discourse with another, or read a book, pamphlet, or paper, printed or manuscript. And of two members rising to speak at the same time, the president shall name him who shall be first heard."

The next day, May 29, the delegates adopted the rule that all proceedings should be kept secret. This rule was made to avoid adding fuel to the public speculation about what was happening at the convention. Many points of view would be presented during the debates, many of which would have nothing to do with the final proposals. The delegates decided that the final results should be judged on their own merits, without reference to the arguments, disagreements, and compromises that went into it. Secrecy also assured the delegates that they could speak freely, without concern for reaction in the press or in public opinion.

The secrecy rule did not apply only to the actual time of the convention. The detailed accounts of the actual debates, as they were recorded by James Madison, remained secret for fifty years. They were not made known to the American public until 1840, after Madison's death.

On the same day that the secrecy rule was adopted, Edmund Randolph, of the Virginia delegation, opened the debate with a slate of fifteen resolutions. These became known as the "Virginia Plan," and they formed the basis for almost all discussion at the convention.

The first of the fifteen resolutions was in keeping with the stated purpose of the convention: "that the Articles of Confederation ought to be so corrected and enlarged as to accomplish the objects proposed by their institution, namely common defense, security of liberty, and general welfare." It should be remembered that this was all that the delegates to the convention were supposed to do. The writing of a new constitution was not the original intent of the convention, and a few states had sent delegates with the stipulation that they take part only in revising the Articles.

The next day, the convention went into

Virginia State Library

Edmund Randolph, governor of Virginia, presented the "Virginia Plan" at the convention.

a "committee of the whole" in order to discuss Randolph's proposals more freely. With a swiftness that would not characterize the rest of the convention, the delegates came to a major decision. They voted to adopt the third of Randolph's fifteen resolutions: "that a national government ought to be established, consisting of a supreme legislative, executive, and judiciary."

This accomplished two extremely important ends. First, it made the concept of forming a "national government" the basis of the debate, rather than mere revision

The Virginia Plan as revised after its initial presentation at the convention. In this version, the original Resolution 1, that the Articles of Confederation ought to be "corrected," has been dropped, and the resolutions have been renumbered.

State of the resolutions submitted to the consideration of the House by the honorable Mr. Randolph, as altered, amended, and agreed to in a Committee of the whole House.

1. Resolved
p. 2
4 p. 26

that it is the opinion of this Committee that a national government ought to be established consisting of
a Supreme Legislative, Judiciary, and Executive.

2. Resolved.
4 3.

That the national Legislature ought to consist of
Two Branches.

3. Resolved

That the members of the first branch of the national Legislature ought to be elected by
the People of the several States
for the term of Three years.
to receive fixed stipends, by which they may be compensated for the devotion of their time to public service
to be paid out of the National Treasury.
to be ineligible to any Office established by a particular State or under the authority of the United States (except those peculiarly belonging to the functions of the first branch) during the term of service, and under the national government for the space of one year after it's expiration.

4. Resolved.

That the members of the second branch of the national Legislature ought to be chosen by
the individual Legislatures.
to be of the age of thirty years at least.
to hold their offices for a term sufficient to ensure their independency, namely seven years.
to receive fixed stipends, by which they may be compensated for the devotion of their time to public service — to be paid out of the national Treasury
to be ineligible to any office established by a particular State, or under the authority of the United States (except those peculiarly belonging to the functions of the second branch) during the term of service, and under the national government, for the space of One year after it's expiration.

6

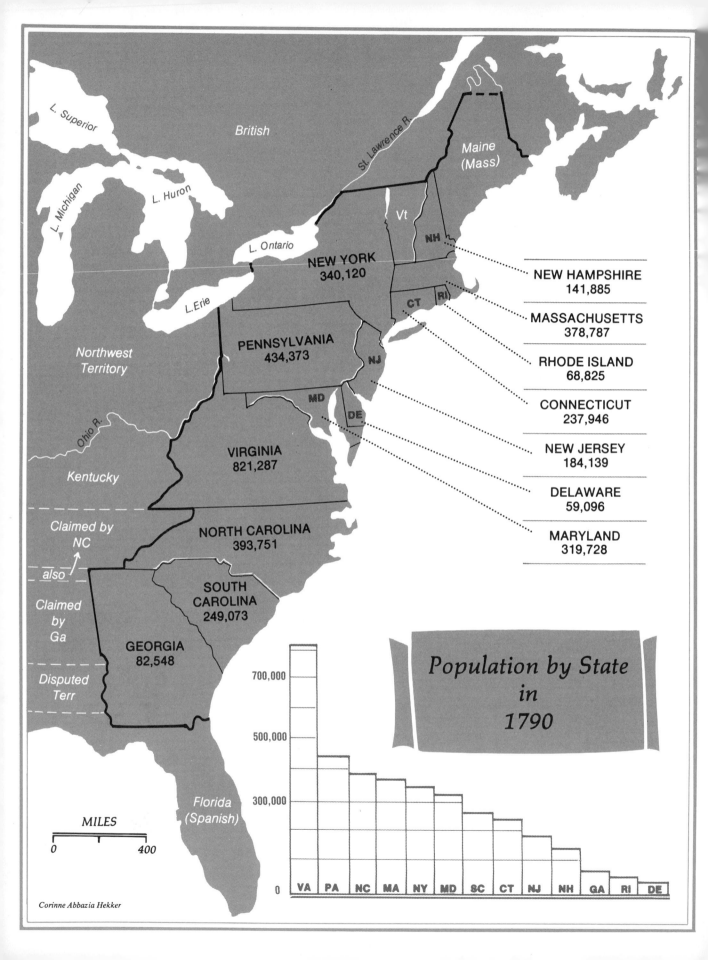

L. Superior

British

L. Michigan

L. Huron

St. Lawrence R.

Maine (Mass)

L. Ontario

Vt

NH

NEW YORK
340,120

Northwest Territory

L. Erie

CT

RI)

NEW HAMPSHIRE
141,885

PENNSYLVANIA
434,373

NJ

MASSACHUSETTS
378,787

RHODE ISLAND
68,825

Ohio R.

MD

CONNECTICUT
237,946

Kentucky

VIRGINIA
821,287

DE

NEW JERSEY
184,139

DELAWARE
59,096

Claimed by
NC

MARYLAND
319,728

NORTH CAROLINA
393,751

also

Claimed
by
Ga

SOUTH
CAROLINA
249,073

Disputed
Terr

GEORGIA
82,548

*Population by State
in
1790*

700,000

500,000

300,000

Florida
(Spanish)

MILES

0   400

0

VA | PA | NC | MA | NY | MD | SC | CT | NJ | NH | GA | RI | DE

Corinne Abbazia Hekker

of the Articles of Confederation. Second, it approved the principle of a "three-branch government."

The three-branch system, as outlined in 1748 by the French philosopher Baron de Montesquieu, was considered the wisest and safest method of government. The purpose for the division of responsibilities was twofold. First, it separated powers so that no branch would hold ultimate control. Second, it allowed each branch to check the power of the other two. The specific "checks and balances" had yet to be worked out at the convention, but the principle was established at the outset.

The idea of the separation of powers echoes the belief that people are corrupted by power. To lessen the chances of corruption and tyranny, each of the three branches is given specific powers. These powers are protected against attempts by the other branches to undermine them. At the same time, however, each branch has a check on the other two to keep them within certain limits.

The agreement among the delegates that the national government should consist of three branches created the skeleton of a constitution. The convention still had to put flesh on the bones: It had to decide what powers each branch would have. This involved deciding the degree to which the national government would have power over the states—a touchy issue. Also remaining was the question of how representation in the government would be divided between the large and small states.

The latter point was one of the most difficult that the convention had to resolve.

Under the Articles of Confederation, each state had one vote, and each state was virtually an independent country. This created a problem in that smaller states were on equal footing with larger states, and the larger states feared that their interests would be undermined by equal representation of all states in a national government. The smaller states feared that representation that was proportional to population would result in their being dominated by the larger states.

UPI/Bettmann Archive

The French philosopher Montesquieu, whose 1748 treatise The Spirit of Laws *greatly influenced the framing of the Constitution*

Many other points would have to be decided as well. The way the convention worked, issues were debated, and if no agreement could be reached, they would be put aside for future discussion. The best way to understand the work of the convention is to look at the major arguments and compromises that went into settling the larger questions for each of the three branches of government.

The Legislature

The first important decision made at the convention about the legislature was that it should consist of two branches This is known as a "bicameral legislature." (The word "bicameral" is derived from Latin and means "having two chambers.")

Although it was yet to be decided, the delegates assumed that this division would consist of an "upper" and a "lower" house. The upper house would be smaller, more exclusive, and representative of the more established interests of society. The lower house would tend to be larger and more representative of the people as a whole.

The first major debate on the legislature concerned how the larger, or lower, house was to be elected. This was really a debate on whether or not the people should elect their representatives directly. The alternative was for them to be elected by the state legislatures. The delegates who favored the latter method were concerned about an "excess of democracy." They believed that the people were too easily deceived by "pretended patriots" and that they were often misled by false reports of events.

Those in favor of direct election argued that the interests of the people should form the base of the federal government. The government, they insisted, would be strengthened by the direct involvement of the people, who would be more likely to give their support to something they had participated in.

Most of the delegates agreed with this second view, and a vote decided the question in favor of direct election of the larger house by the people. This issue was reopened later, and more arguments were presented for election by the state legisla-

National Portrait Gallery

Gouverneur Morris, delegate from New York, supported the creation of a strong central government.

tures. But a motion in favor of this method was defeated. Direct election to the House of Representatives by the people was thereby reaffirmed.

The next important question was how the upper house, the Senate, would be elected. Several methods were suggested. Since the people would elect the lower house directly, the delegates decided that the state legislatures should appoint the senators. The idea that state governments should be responsible for electing part of the national government reaffirmed the power of the states as political units. The practice of state legislatures' electing senators, which might seem odd to us today, continued until 1913, when the 17th Amendment to the Constitution transferred the responsibility for electing senators directly to the people.

Once the *method* of election to the two houses of Congress was determined, the delegates had to decide the question of representation. In other words, would each state have an equal number of representatives or would membership be proportional to state population? Or should representation be based on some other factor, such as a state's total wealth?

The debate on this issue remained at a deadlock for some time. Eventually, however, the delegates from large and small states reached what is called the "Great Compromise." They decided that each state would be represented in the House of Representatives in proportion to its population, whereas in the Senate, each state would be represented by two members, regardless of population. Thus, room had

been made for the two main opposing points of view: that of the larger states, which wanted representation to be based on the number of people in a state, and that of the smaller states, which wanted representation to be based on the equality of the states as sovereign political units.

The fundamental issue that had led to the Revolution had been the objection by the Colonies to taxes levied by the British Parliament. It is no coincidence, therefore, that the power to originate tax legislation was placed in the House of Representatives.

The Constitution is essentially a series of balancing acts. The legislative branch was given the great power to make national laws, to make the United States a solid, governable republic. The power to enforce the laws, the power of everyday governance, however, was placed in the hands of another branch, the executive.

The Executive

When the debate on the executive branch began, no delegate was sure how that office should be set up. Some delegates feared that if the executive were given too much power, an uncontrollable tyranny would be the result. Others feared that giving the executive too little power would result in a lack of leadership.

The debates at first centered on whether the executive should consist of one man or a committee of three men. Those in favor of a committee argued that if each of the three executives was chosen from a different region of the country, each region would receive due consideration in all important decisions. Those in favor of a single executive argued that one man, representing all interests, would be able to govern most effectively. A committee elected regionally might get bogged down in regional disputes. As a result, the national interest would suffer. The latter argument prevailed, and the convention voted for the concept of a single executive, to be called the president of the United States.

Another major question was the length of the president's term of office. Some delegates felt that for a president to be an effective leader, he must serve for life, or at least for a term of fifteen or twenty years. But the opponents of this view argued that the president should be more accountable to his electors. Various delegates favored a three-year term, a six-year term, and a seven-year term.

The final compromise called for a four-year term. A good argument can be made that this was a wise choice. Four years turns out to be just enough time for a president to establish leadership and enact programs that can then be tested by a new election. If the electors decide that the president has been ineffective, another candidate can be elected.

The most sensitive issue concerning the presidency was the method of election. It must be remembered that democracy, the direct participation of the people, was a prospect that frightened many of the delegates. This was not a feeling based in a dislike of the people as a whole but rather in the honest fear that people were easily deceived and manipulated.

Some delegates argued for direct election by the people, whereas others proposed that it be done by the state legislatures. Three other methods were proposed. One called for the president to be elected by both houses of Congress; another, by the Senate alone; and another, by the governors of the states.

The final decision created one of the oddities of the American system, what has come to be known as the "Electoral College." Each state selects a number of presidential electors equal to the number of representatives and senators from that state. These electors then vote for president. In the Constitution as ratified in 1789, the candidate receiving the greatest number of electoral votes became president and the candidate with the second-highest total became the vice-president. This was changed by the 12th Amendment, in 1803, so that candidates ran either for president or for vice-president.

Today, the candidate who wins the popular vote in a state receives all of that state's electoral votes. This is not specified in the Constitution, however, and the Electoral College is a source of controversy to this day. In case of a tie in the electoral vote, the Constitution specifies that the election shall be decided in the House of Representatives.

If the Constitutional Convention took pains to decide the term of office and the

Benjamin Franklin, eighty-one years old at the time of the convention, was largely responsible for the Great Compromise that led to ratification.

Articles of Confederation

ARTICLE V. For the more convenient management of the general interests of the United States, delegates [to Congress] shall be annually appointed in such manner as the legislature of each state shall direct.... No state shall be represented in Congress by less than two nor by more than seven members. ... In determining questions in the United States in Congress assembled, each state shall have one vote.

U.S. Constitution (with the Bill of Rights)

ARTICLE I, SECTION 1. All legislative powers herein granted shall be vested in a Congress of the United States, which shall consist of a Senate and House of Representatives. .... *SECTION 2.* Representatives and direct taxes shall be apportioned among the several states ... according to their respective numbers.

Here the Constitution broadly revises the structure of Congress and establishes two crucial institutions: the bicameral (two-chambered) legislature, with its Senate and House borrowed directly from Britain's House of Lords and House of Commons; and *proportional* representation, to supplant the "one vote per state" rule that characterized the Confederation.

ARTICLE VIII. All charges of war and all other expenses that shall be incurred for the common defense or general welfare ... shall be defrayed out of a common treasury, which shall be supplied by the several states in proportion to the value of all land within each state ... The taxes for paying that proportion shall be laid and levied by the authority and direction of the legislatures of the several states within the time agreed upon by the United States in Congress assembled.

ARTICLE I, SECTION 8. The Congress shall have power to lay and collect taxes, duties, imposts, and excises, to pay the debts and provide for the common defense and general welfare of the United States.

In perhaps the most important measure passed at the Constitutional Convention, Congress is granted the power of direct taxation of individuals.

Articles of Confederation

ARTICLE VII. When land forces are raised by any state for the common defense, all officers of or under the rank of colonel shall be appointed by the legislature of each state respectively, by whom such forces shall be raised, or in such manner as such state shall direct.

U.S. Constitution (with the Bill of Rights)

ARTICLE II, SECTION 1. The executive power shall be vested in a President of the United States of America. . . . *SECTION 2.* The President shall be commander in chief of the Army and Navy of the United States, and of the militia of the several states when called into the actual service of the United States . . . *ARTICLE I, SECTION 8.* [The Congress shall have power] to provide for organizing, arming, and disciplining the militia and for governing such part of them as may be employed in the service of the United States.

Article II of the Constitution not only establishes the executive branch of government but makes its chief executive, the president, the highest-ranking officer in the military. Earlier, in Article I, the Constitution further weakens the Confederation's system of independent state militias by granting Congress the power to finance and organize the militias as they saw fit for the common defense, or the national good.

ARTICLE II. Each state retains its sovereignty, freedom, and independence, and every power, jurisdiction, and right which is not by this confederation expressly delegated to the United States in Congress assembled.

AMENDMENT X. The powers not delegated to the United States by the Constitution, nor prohibited by it to the states, are reserved to the states respectively, or to the people.

Note that although these two clauses seek to achieve the same end, what was under the Articles a declaration of state sovereignty became in the Constitution a concession of rights not delegated—or not *yet* delegated—to the federal government. In the end, the assertion of central or federal authority was most clearly stated in the Constitution's Article VI, in the so-called supremacy clause, which states, in part, "This Constitution and the laws of the United States . . . shall be the supreme law of the land; and the judges in every state shall be bound thereby, anything in the constitution or laws of any state to the contrary notwithstanding."

New York Public Library

James Wilson, of Pennsylvania, was responsible for much of the language of the finished constitution.

method of election of the president, it was even more careful in designating presidential powers. The president would be allowed to veto laws passed by Congress, but Congress could, in turn, override (or nullify) the veto by a two-thirds vote in each house.

The president was given the power to make treaties with foreign governments, but only with the advice and consent of the Senate. Likewise, the delegates agreed that the president should be commander in chief of the armed forces, but the power to declare war was placed in the hands of Congress. In addition, the president would have the right to grant executive pardons, and he would be subject to impeachment and removal from office for "treason, bribery and other high crimes and misdemeanors."

Some historians have reasoned that the convention decided on a strong presidency because they were shaping it to fit the character and leadership abilities of George Washington. It was generally accepted by the delegates that Washington would, indeed, be the first president. It would not be unfair to say, therefore, that from the start, the presidency was meant to be occupied by a "great man," which Washington certainly was.

Thus, the delegates had outlined the duties of the first two branches of government: the making of laws by the legislature and the administration of those laws by the executive. Now came the very different design of the third branch, the judiciary, which would interpret the laws and pass ultimate judgment in legal disputes.

The Judiciary

Even as they were deciding the structure of the Constitution, the delegates knew that it would serve only as a broad guideline for the new republic. The Constitution was to be a format in which laws were created, executive decisions were made, and through which justice would be preserved. The delegates also realized that many of the mechanics of the new government would have to be worked out in practice.

A great deal of time was spent during the convention working out the size, shape, and powers of the legislative branch. Somewhat less time was devoted to laying out the boundaries of the presidency. But the least time of all was devoted to outlining the judiciary. Essentially, all that was decided was that the judicial power would be embodied in a supreme court. That court would consist of judges appointed by the president and approved by the Senate. It would be responsible for hearing and passing judgments in legal cases on the national level.

The number of justices who would sit on the court was not specified. Nor were there any specifications as to how the court would function or make rules for itself.

The federal judiciary, in particular the Supreme Court, is the branch of government most removed from the influence of the people. Unless a justice commits a crime or other breach of trust, he serves for life. The Congress can impeach justices, but neither the Congress nor the president can overrule or veto a decision by the Court.

The only way Congress can correct what it believes to be a poor or improper decision by the Court is to pass a new law. But the Court might still rule that the new law is unconstitutional. The only method for correcting the Court, in that case, would be for a new amendment to be added to the Constitution. Amending the Constitution is a difficult process: A proposed amendment must be ratified first by two thirds of the members of both houses of Congress, then by at least three fourths of the states themselves.

Therefore, short of a constitutional amendment, the Supreme Court is the final judge in disputes, and as such it holds the most unchecked power of the three branches of government. Depending on the point of view, this can be seen as either a blessing or a curse. The controversy over the Court's considerable power continues to this day.

It was decided late in the convention that the Constitution would take effect if and when it had been ratified by nine of the thirteen states. Final changes were made, and a committee on style reworked the document so that it would read and sound consistent in composition.

When it came time for the delegates to sign the proposed constitution, the aged Benjamin Franklin took the floor and urged them to give their approval. He said, in part, "I confess that there are several parts of the Constitution which I do not at present approve, but I am not sure I shall never approve them. For having lived long, I have experienced many instances of being obliged by better information or fuller consideration to change opinions, even on important subjects, which I once thought right, but found to be otherwise. It is, therefore, that the older I grow the more apt I am to doubt my own judgment and to pay more respect to the judgment of others. On the whole, sir, I cannot help expressing a wish that every member of the convention, who may still have objections to it, would with me on this occasion doubt a little of his own infallibility, and to make manifest our unanimity put his name to this instrument."

National Archives

Overleaf: Detail from the Constitution

We the People

of the ...

... secure domestic Tranquility, provide for the common defence, ...
... and our Posterity, do ordain and establish this Constitution for ...

Article

Section 1. All legislative Powers herein granted, shall be vested ...
... Representatives.

Section 2. The House of Representatives shall be composed of ...
in each State shall have the Qualifications requisite for Electors of the most nu...

No Person shall be a Representative who shall not have attain...
... who shall not, when elected, be an Inhabitant of that State in which ...

Representatives and direct Taxes shall be apportioned among the ...
Numbers, which shall be determined by adding to the whole Number of f...
not taxed, three fifths of all other Persons. The actual Enumeration sh...
and within every subsequent Term of ten Years, in such Manner as they ...
thirty thousand, but each State shall have at Least one Representative ...
entitled to chuse three, Massachusetts eight, Rhode-Island and Provi...
eight, Delaware one, Maryland six, Virginia ten, North Carolina fi...

When vacancies happen in the Representation from any Stat...
The House of Representatives shall chuse their Speaker and oth...

Section 3. The Senate of the United States shall be composed of two ...
Senator shall have one Vote.

Immediately after they shall be assembled in Consequence of ...
of the Senators of the first Class shall be vacated at the Expiration of the ...
Class at the Expiration of the sixth Year, so that one third may be chosen ...
Recess of the Legislature of any State, the Executive thereof may make temp...
such Vacancies.

No Person shall be a Senator who shall not have attained to the ...
not, when elected, be an Inhabitant of that State for which he shall be ch...

The Vice President of the United States shall be President of their ...

States, in Order to form a more perfect Union, establish Justice,
general Welfare, and secure the Blessings of Liberty to ourselves
States of America.

Congress of the United States, which shall consist of a Senate and House

chosen every second Year by the People of the several States, and the Electors
Branch of the State Legislature.
Age of twenty five Years, and been seven Years a Citizen of the United States,
be chosen.
States which may be included within this Union, according to their respective
including those bound to Service for a Term of Years, and excluding Indians
made within three Years after the first Meeting of the Congress of the United States,
Law direct. The Number of Representatives shall not exceed one for every
until such enumeration shall be made, the State of New Hampshire shall be
Plantations one, Connecticut five, New York six, New Jersey four, Pennsylvania
Carolina five, and Georgia three.
cutive Authority thereof shall issue Writs of Election to fill such Vacancies.
; and shall have the sole Power of Impeachment.
from each State, chosen by the Legislature thereof, for six Years; and each

Election, they shall be divided as equally as may be into three Classes. The Seats
Year, of the second Class at the Expiration of the fourth Year, and of the third
second Year; and if Vacancies happen by Resignation, or otherwise, during the
appointments until the next Meeting of the Legislature, which shall then fill

thirty Years, and been nine Years a Citizen of the United States, and who shall

shall have no Vote, unless they be equally divided.
Vice President, or when he shall exercise the Office of

4

THE BATTLE OVER RATIFICATION

The drama that surrounded the Constitutional Convention did not end when the delegates left Philadelphia in September of 1787, some four months after they first convened. The thirteen states would now have to consider the new constitution in their individual ratifying conventions. The Constitution had many vigorous opponents, and it was not clear that it would gain the approval of enough states to be enacted.

During this crucial period, late 1787 and early 1788, three men wrote eighty-five essays that attempted to explain, justify, and defend the Constitution. Alexander Hamilton, James Madison, and John Jay would all achieve honored places in American history. Collected in a single volume, their essays were titled *The Federalist* (also known as *The Federalist Papers*), and are recognized as the greatest American contribution to the history of political thought.

One of the most interesting facts about *The Federalist* is that Hamilton, who wrote at least fifty-one of the essays, had spoken against the republican form of government at the convention. Hamilton had favored the establishment of a stronger central government, in the form of a "parliamentary monarchy," such as that of Great Britain. Only after the convention did he take up the cause of the Constitution and the republic that it would create. He believed that the strength the delegates had given to the national government was far preferable to the shallow unity established by the Articles of Confederation. Originally published in newspapers in New York, the essays were bound together for use at the state conventions, as ammunition for those favoring ratification.

The first state to ratify the Constitution was Delaware, which did so unanimously

James Madison, principal architect of the Constitution and, later, of the Bill of Rights

New York Historical Society

National Portrait Gallery

Alexander Hamilton, author of much of The Federalist *and the nation's first Secretary of the Treasury*

There was strong sentiment against the Constitution in all three states, and because of their vital importance, the failure of any of the three to ratify could seriously injure the prospects of a new government under the Constitution.

The first big test came at the Massachusetts convention. The debate was fierce, with those for and against vigorously arguing their positions. In the end, Massachusetts voted for ratification, but the vote was close, 187 delegates voting yes, 168 no.

Following the Massachusetts vote, Maryland voted to ratify on April 2, and South Carolina approved on May 23. Then, in early June 1788, came the Virginia convention. The most intense of all the ratifying debates took place here. Patrick Henry, one of the great orators of the time, was passionately opposed to the Constitution. He had refused to be a delegate to the convention in Philadelphia, and he ardently believed that the Articles of Confederation should be retained. He was certain that they were a sounder foundation for a more democratic form of government. Most important, Henry argued, the Articles preserved the sovereignty of the individual states and therefore were less of a threat to the independence of the United States and of his beloved Virginia in particular.

Opposing Henry was the soft-spoken James Madison. Though his oratory did not approach Henry's, Madison was a great scholar of politics and government. His calm, self-assured defense of the Constitution contrasted favorably with Henry's

on December 7, 1787. That very small state was clearly satisfied with the establishment of the Senate, in which it would have representation equal with that of much larger states. Pennsylvania became the second state to ratify, on December 12. The New Jersey convention approved unanimously on December 18, and Georgia ratified on January 2, 1788.

The rapid approval of these four states was encouraging to supporters of the Constitution. But the big challenge in the three most important states—Massachusetts, New York, and Virginia—was yet to come.

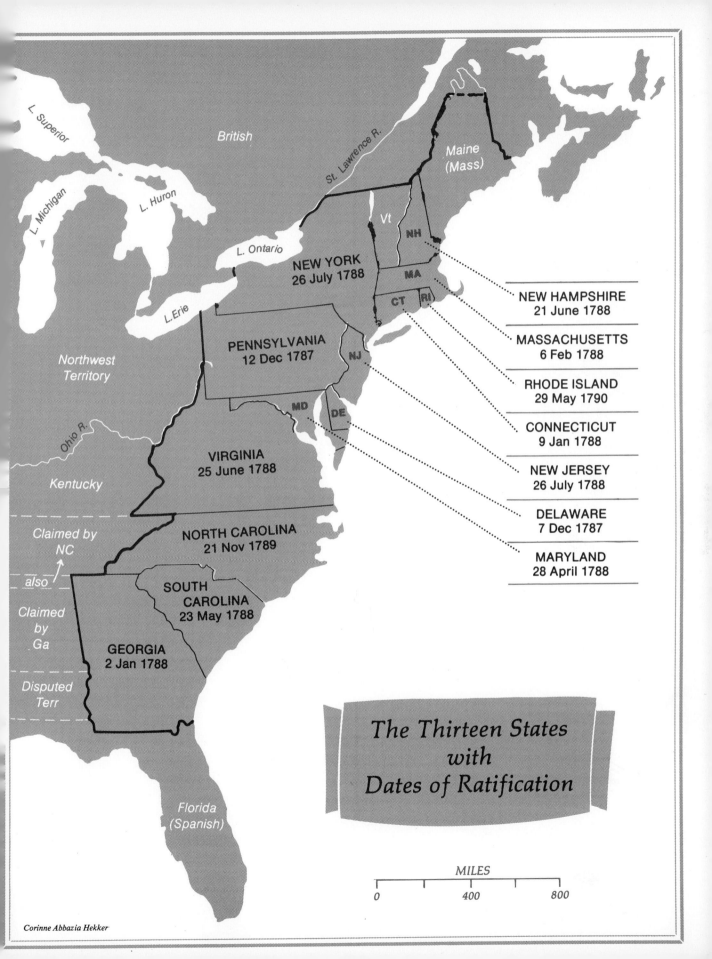

L. Superior

British

L. Michigan

L. Huron

Northwest
Territory

L. Ontario

L. Erie

St. Lawrence R.

Maine
(Mass)

Vt

NH

NEW YORK
26 July 1788

MA

CT

RI

Ohio R.

PENNSYLVANIA
12 Dec 1787

NJ

Kentucky

MD

DE

VIRGINIA
25 June 1788

Claimed by
NC

also

NORTH CAROLINA
21 Nov 1789

Claimed
by
Ga

SOUTH
CAROLINA
23 May 1788

GEORGIA
2 Jan 1788

Disputed
Terr

Florida
(Spanish)

NEW HAMPSHIRE
21 June 1788

MASSACHUSETTS
6 Feb 1788

RHODE ISLAND
29 May 1790

CONNECTICUT
9 Jan 1788

NEW JERSEY
26 July 1788

DELAWARE
7 Dec 1787

MARYLAND
28 April 1788

The Thirteen States
with
Dates of Ratification

MILES

0   400   800

Corinne Abbazia Hekker

National Portrait Gallery

John Jay, coauthor of The Federalist *and the first chief justice of the Supreme Court*

REDEUNT SATURNIA REGNA.

On the erection of the Eleventh PILLAR of the great Na-

tional DOME, *we beg leave most sincerely to felicitate* " OUR DEAR COUNTRY."

Rise it will.

The foundation good—it may yet be SAVED

The FEDERAL EDIFICE.

ELEVEN STARS, in quick succession rise—
ELEVEN COLUMNS strike our wond'ring eyes,
Soon o'er the *whole*, shall swell the beauteous DOME,
COLUMBIA's boast—and FREEDOM's hallow'd home.
    Here shall the ARTS in glorious splendour shine !
And AGRICULTURE give her stores divine !
COMMERCE refin'd, dispense us more than gold,
And this new world, teach WISDOM to the old—
RELIGION here shall fix her blest abode,
Array'd in *mildness*, like its parent GOD !
JUSTICE and LAW, shall endless PEACE maintain,
And *the* " SATURNIAN AGE," *return again.*

Cartoon from the Massachusetts Centinel *celebrating the erection of the "eleventh pillar"—New York State—in the "federal edifice." The toppling pillars at right represent North Carolina and Rhode Island, the two states yet to ratify at the time.*

passionate but long-winded attack.

Perhaps the greatest blow to Henry and the other Virginia delegates opposed to the Constitution was delivered by Edmund Randolph. Randolph had been one of the three delegates present at the end of the Philadelphia convention who had refused to sign the finished Constitution. He told the Virginia convention that he had not signed because the Constitution did not contain a guarantee of basic rights. He was willing to support ratification with the condition that amendments be added that protected these rights.

In the final vote, the Virginia convention ratified the Constitution by a vote of 89 to 79. But while the Virginians had been debating, New Hampshire quietly became the ninth state to ratify, thus giving the Constitution the number of votes it needed in order to be adopted. Still, as proponents of the document knew all along, mere passage of the Constitution would not guarantee that it would endure.

The last important battle was yet to be fought: New York had still not ratified.

As a prosperous state with a large population, New York was vital to the Union,

47

Hamiltonians, Jeffersonians and James Madison

With the installation of the new government under the Constitution in 1789, many long-standing political differences of opinion sharpened. There arose out of these differences two distinct political "camps" and, thus, the beginning of the nation's traditional two-party system. The story of the Hamiltonian Federalists versus the Jeffersonian Democratic Republicans is perhaps best told through the career of one founding father, one of the younger among them and perhaps the new republic's most brilliant political philosopher, James Madison.

Madison graduated from the College of New Jersey (now Princeton) at the age of twenty, in 1771, and in 1776 helped draft the constitution of the state of Virginia. From 1780 to 1786 he served in the Continental Congress and in the Virginia legislature, and by the latter year he was convinced that the central government, under the Articles of Confederation, needed strengthening. Although an admirer and political ally of his fellow Virginian Thomas Jefferson, Madison sided with Alexander Hamilton and other Federalists in supporting passage of a constitutionally stronger federal government. (Jefferson himself did not oppose passage but was wary of the Federalists' intentions.) Once ratification of the Constitution seemed ensured, however, Madison began to part ways with his former allies Hamilton and Jay and to urge amendment of the Constitution in the form of a bill of rights. Madison was now on his way back, so to speak, to his local, states' rights, democratic roots.

By the end of Washington's first term, in 1792, Congressman Madison was one of the leaders of the Jeffersonian Democratic Republican party, who were opposed to the Washington administration's further strengthening of federal authority. Then, in 1798, came the biggest split yet. The Federalists, under President John Adams, passed a series of measures known as the Alien and Sedition Acts. The laws—particularly those dealing with "sedition" (words or acts that might lead to treason)—were seen by the Jeffersonians as meant to punish newspaper editors sympathetic with the Democratic Republican opposition in Congress. In response, Jefferson and Madison undertook the severe measure of drafting the Kentucky and Virginia Resolutions, which declared that the federal sedition laws were null and void in the sovereign states of Kentucky and Virginia.

Public reaction against the Alien and Sedition Acts led to the defeat of the Federalists in 1800, the election of Jefferson as the nation's third president, and, in turn, the presidency of James Madison himself, beginning in 1809. Still, it is in the career of James Madison prior to his presidency that we see lived out a central struggle of American political life; that is, the coexistence of governmental authority with personal, individual freedom.

New York Public Library

John Lansing

but it was also a hotbed of anti-Constitutionalists. The ratification debates were heated and dramatic. Alexander Hamilton, the only New York delegate to the Philadelphia convention who had signed the Constitution, led the fight for ratification. He was opposed by New York's very popular former governor, George Clinton. Also opposed were two men who had been in Philadelphia and who had quit the convention in frustration: Robert Yates and John Lansing.

As with Virginia, the greatest concern of the New Yorkers who opposed the Constitution was its lack of a bill of rights. When a vote was finally taken, after weeks of deliberation, many of the delegates voted to ratify only on the assurance that a bill of rights would be amended to the Constitution. New York's vote was 31 yes, 29 no, a close victory for the Constitution. But approval by New York, the eleventh state to ratify, meant that the new Union had at least a fighting chance.

North Carolina did not ratify the Constitution until November of 1788. And Rhode Island—the only state that had not sent a representative to the convention—would not ratify until 1790. But by the middle of 1788, preparations had begun for the establishment of the new federal government.

On February 4, 1789, George Washington was unanimously chosen as the first president of the United States by the Electoral College. Some unfortunate delays prevented an immediate official count of the vote. But on April 30, 1789, the man for whom the presidency was made took the oath of office before both houses of Congress at Federal Hall in New York City.

AFTERWORD

THE LIVING CONSTITUTION

The new United States of America, with its new constitution, began with only one assurance that it would survive its first few years. That assurance was the leadership of George Washington.

It was said that what enthusiasm the people initially had for the new government came from the knowledge that Washington would be at the head of it. The old general breathed life into the republic simply by being there.

The first important action of the new federal government was for Congress to set about drafting the Bill of Rights. Many of the state ratifying conventions had approved the Constitution in anticipation of amendments that guaranteed basic liberties. And there was another voice—a very strong one—pleading in favor of a bill of

John Marshall, chief justice of the Supreme Court from 1801 to 1835. The right of the Court to judge the constitutionality of federal and state laws—never spelled out in the Constitution itself—was established by Marshall and his court.

rights: that of Thomas Jefferson, U.S. minister to France, who was in Paris at the time of the convention. Jefferson was kept informed of the events in Philadelphia by his close friend James Madison, and though mail was slow to cross the Atlantic in the eighteenth century, Jefferson's comments on the proposed constitution were dated as early as December of 1787. They included his belief that the president should not be eligible for a second four-year term, but this was not a major objection. What was most important to Jefferson was the inclusion of a bill of rights in the Constitution.

Debates over the amendments in Congress lasted some three and a half months. Eventually, a group of eight amendments, written by James Madison, was submitted as the Bill of Rights. Amendments Nine and Ten stated basically that any rights *not* specifically mentioned in the first eight amendments were nonetheless guaranteed to the people and to the states. These final two amendments, though not originally

National Portrait Gallery

New York Public Library

The first inauguration of George Washington, at Federal Hall in New York City, April 30, 1789. At Washington's left is John Adams, first vice-president of the U.S.

submitted as part of the Bill of Rights, were ratified along with the first eight and are properly considered part of the Bill.

The Bill of Rights was ratified by the states and became part of the Constitution in December 1791. These amendments serve to protect the people against encroachment on their basic liberties by the federal government. They guarantee, for example, freedom of speech, religion, and the press (First Amendment). They protect people against unreasonable searches of their homes and seizure of their property (Fourth). They provide for due process of law (Fifth) and a fair and speedy trial by jury (Sixth and Seventh). They protect convicted criminals against excessive bail and cruel and unusual punishment (Eighth).

Though the Bill of Rights reassured the people about the intentions of their new government, it did not ensure that the government itself would survive. There was no republic on earth that had gone so far in trying to satisfy the interests of so many different sectors of its population.

CONGRESS OF THE UNITED STATES.

In the House of Representatives,

Monday, 24th August, 1789.

RESOLVED, by the Senate and House of Representatives of the United States of America in Congress assembled, two thirds of both Houses deeming it necessary, That the following Articles be proposed to the Legislatures of the several States, as Amendments to the Constitution of the United States, all or any of which Articles, when ratified by three fourths of the said Legislatures, to be valid to all intents and purposes as part of the said Constitution—Viz.

ARTICLES in addition to, and amendment of, the Constitution of the United States of America, proposed by Congress, and ratified by the Legislatures of the several States, pursuant to the fifth Article of the original Constitution.

ARTICLE THE FIRST.

After the first enumeration, required by the first Article of the Constitution, there shall be one Representative for every thirty thousand, until the number shall amount to one hundred, after which the proportion shall be so regulated by Congress, that there shall be not less than one hundred Representatives, nor less than one Representative for every forty thousand persons, until the number of Representatives shall amount to two hundred, after which the proportion shall be so regulated by Congress, that there shall not be less than two hundred Representatives, nor less than one Representative for every fifty thousand persons.

ARTICLE THE SECOND.

No law varying the compensation to the members of Congress, shall take effect, until an election of Representatives shall have intervened.

ARTICLE THE THIRD.

Congress shall make no law establishing religion or prohibiting the free exercise thereof, nor shall the rights of Conscience be infringed.

ARTICLE THE FOURTH.

The Freedom of Speech, and of the Press, and the right of the People peaceably to assemble, and to apply to the Government for a redress of grievances, shall not be infringed.

Working copy of an early version of the Bill of Rights submitted to the Senate for ratification in August 1789. This version included twelve amendments, the first two of which were never ratified.

Time would tell whether such a great degree of liberty would spill over into chaos and strife.

It is to Washington's first term that the origins of the two-party system can be traced. This came about because of two great men Washington asked to join his first cabinet. As his first Secretary of State, Washington chose Thomas Jefferson, the author of the Declaration of Independence. To the important cabinet post of Secretary of the Treasury the first president appointed Alexander Hamilton, his former chief of staff during the Revolution.

It was the clash between these two men and their very different ideas that led to the development of opposing political parties when Washington left office. It was Washington's even-handed mediation of this clash, however, that made room for the ideas of both men in the new republic.

Jefferson was the great proponent of democracy. He believed in the people and their natural talent and goodness. He

President Washington and his first cabinet. Left to right are Henry Knox, Secretary of War; Alexander Hamilton, Secretary of the Treasury; Thomas Jefferson, Secretary of State; and Edmund Randolph, Attorney General.

Private Collection

New York Public Library

The first Bank of the United States, in Philadelphia, became a symbol to anti-Federalists of the new central government's intention to control matters of finance, trade, and taxation.

greatly admired the vitality of the French Revolution. The party that Jefferson founded was the "Republican" or "Democratic Republican" party, the ancestor of the Democratic Party of the present century.

Hamilton was a proponent of a less-democratic, more elite form of republican government. He did not believe that the people were endowed with natural wisdom, and he feared the consequences of

the French Revolution. Hamilton promoted the interests of businessmen and financiers and as Secretary of the Treasury established the Bank of the United States. He believed that success in commerce and industry was the best hope for the new republic. The party that formed around those ideas became known as the Federalist Party. The Federalist Party faded out during the early 1800s, but some of Hamilton's ideas about the importance of commercial interests are reflected in policies favored by the Republican Party of today.

Washington saw the good points on both sides. He did lean more toward the Federalist point of view in his second term, but that seems to have been a wise reaction to popular "democratic societies," grass-roots political organizations of that time that wanted to push America more toward France and the ideas of its revolution. (The French Revolution did indeed end in chaos and terror, and eventually in the rise to power of Napoleon Bonaparte, the military dictator who declared himself emperor.)

One of the truly great contributions made by Washington was, oddly enough, his departure from office. It was when he left the presidency on schedule and an orderly transition took place (John Adams was elected the second president) that the republic proved itself workable. It was a rare moment in the history of the world when a man as great as Washington could step down from a nation's leadership and the ship of state prove able to sail on without him.

So influential was our first president, however, that his farewell address influenced American foreign policy for the next century and a half. In that address, which was published but never actually delivered as a speech, Washington urged the nation to avoid getting involved in European affairs. "The great rule of conduct for us, in regard to foreign nations," Washington wrote, "is in extending our commercial relations to have with them as little political connection as possible."

It can be argued that Washington set the standard for all future presidents. And though men of his caliber do not come to national politics very often, Washington's impact will be felt in the nation's highest office so long as the republic survives.

Another of the issues that Washington raised in his farewell address was that of regional versus national interests. He warned representatives of different regions of the country not to put their interests above those of the nation as a whole. This, he said, would weaken and could ultimately destroy the republic. A half century later, just such a conflict almost destroyed the Union, when eleven Southern states decided to secede and form their own confederation. The bloody disaster known as the Civil War ensued, and the preservation of the Union and of the Constitution was put to its severest test. Following the Union victory in 1865, the rebellious states were restored to the Union. With all the difficulties of this reunion, it was in the end a remarkable achievement, a tribute to the fortitude of Abraham Lincoln and to the durability of the Constitution written nearly eighty years before.

It is ironic that it took one great American tragedy, the Civil War, to bring about the end of another. Since the 1600s, when the states were still raw colonies, black

John Adams, second president of the United States, was, like Washington, a figure of moderation and compromise.

56

Independence National Historical Park Collection

New York Public Library

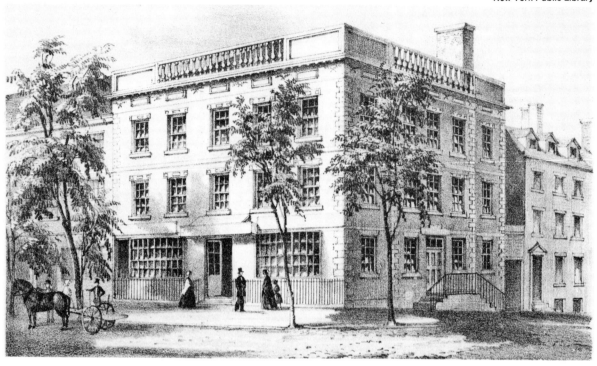

The first presidential mansion, at 1 Cherry Street in New York City. The White House, in Washington, D.C., was not occupied until 1800, the final year of John Adam's presidency.

African men and women had been bound as slaves in America. By the time of the Civil War, slavery still existed in fourteen states, most of them in the South. In spite of all the freedoms to which Americans are entitled, some could still insist that slaves were nothing more than property. In 1863, this great disgrace of American civilization was ended when Lincoln signed the Emancipation Proclamation. To this day, the descendants of former slaves still suffer from the effects of slavery and from ongoing racism, and it is to the guarantees of the Constitution that blacks and other minori-

ties have turned in order to right injustices against them.

Throughout the almost two hundred years that the Constitution has been the law of the land, the Supreme Court has played a very active role in deciding how the Constitution applies to important aspects of American life. The court has helped to define the relationship between church and state. It has handed down numerous rulings on civil rights and liberties, including strict definitions of the rights of people accused of crimes. Over the years, the Court has many times upheld or struck down laws passed by Congress or by the states when these laws have been challenged.

In the almost two hundred years since the ratification of the Constitution, the number of states in the U.S. has increased from thirteen to fifty and the population has grown by approximately six thousand percent, from about 4 million to some 230 million. The nation has also undergone one wrenching civil war, foreign wars great and small, and almost continuous social unrest as ethnic groups new and old strive to take their place in this prosperous land. Still, the work done that summer of 1787—that of providing thirteen relatively small coastal states with a durable central government—has withstood the storms of change and the gentler winds of time, and has left the world with its oldest written charter of government, its words fixed, memorable, their meaning ever arguable, mutable, timeless.

INDEX

Page numbers in *italics* indicate illustrations

SUGGESTED READING

ADAIR, DOUGLAS. *Fame and the Founding Fathers.* New York: Norton, 1974.

ENCYCLOPAEDIA BRITANNICA. *The Annals of America. Volume 3: 1784-1796: Organizing the New Nation.* Chicago, Ill.: Encyclopaedia Britannica, Inc., 1976.

HOFSTADTER, RICHARD, ed. *Great Issues in American History: From the Revolution to the Civil War, 1765-1865.* New York: Vintage, 1958.

JEFFERSON, THOMAS. *Writings.* Merrill Peterson, ed. New York: Library of America, 1983.

KOCH, ADRIENNE. *Madison's Advice to My Country.* Princeton, N.J.: Princeton University Press, 1966.

PROPERTY OF
CHICAGO BOARD OF EDUCATION
DONALD L. MORRILL SCHOOL /

MORRILL ELEMENTARY SCHOOL

34880000805833

342.73
MAC
McPhillips, Martin
    The Constitutional
Convention

DATE DUE			